Mother Bird

Story by Annette Smith   Illustrations by Julian Bruère

Mother Bird is looking

for a worm.

4

Up in the tree,

the baby birds

are hungry.

Mother Bird looks and looks
for a worm.

Here comes a worm.

Mother Bird sees the worm.

Here comes a cat.

The cat sees Mother Bird.

Mother Bird sees the cat.

Up goes Mother Bird.

14

Up, up, up,

goes Mother Bird.

Mother Bird goes up

to the baby birds

in the tree.

The worm

is for the baby birds.